HYMNS IN PROSE FOR CHILDREN.

BY MRS. BARBAULD.

Edited by Sonya Shafer

ILLUSTRATED.

Hymns in Prose for Children

Originally published in 1781 with illustrations added in 1863
By John Murray, Albemarle St.
London

This edition edited by Sonya Shafer
© 2011, Simply Charlotte Mason
All rights reserved.

ISBN: 978-1-61634-144-2 printed
ISBN: 978-1-61634-145-9 electronic download

Published and printed by
Simply Charlotte Mason, LLC
P.O. Box 892
Grayson, Georgia 30017-0892

Cover Design: John Shafer

SimplyCharlotteMason.com

Contents

HYMN I.

COME, let us praise God, for He is exceeding great; let us bless God, for He is very good.

He made all things; the sun to rule the day, the moon to shine by night.

He made the great whale, and the elephant; and the little worm that crawls on the ground.

The little birds sing praises to God, when they warble sweetly in the green shade.

The brooks and rivers praise God, when they murmur melodiously among the smooth pebbles.

Mel o de ous lee

6

I will praise God with my voice; for I may praise Him, though I am but a little child.

A few years ago, and I was a little infant, and my tongue was silent within my mouth:

And I did not know the great name of God, for my reason was not come unto me.

But now I can speak, and my tongue shall praise Him:

I can think of all His kindness, and my heart shall love Him.

Let Him call me, and I will come unto Him: let Him command, and I will obey Him.

When I am older, I will praise Him better, and I will never forget God, so long as my life remains in me.

HYMN II.

Come, let us go into the fields, let us see how the flowers spring, let us listen to the warbling of the birds, and sport ourselves upon the new grass.

The winter is over and gone, the buds come out upon the trees, the crimson blossoms of the peach and the nectarine are seen, and the green leaves sprout.

The hedges are bordered with tufts of primroses, and yellow cowslips that hang down their heads; and the blue violet lies hid beneath the shade.

The young goslings are running upon the green, they are just hatched, their bodies are covered with yellow down; the old ones hiss with anger if anyone comes near.

The hen sits on her nest of straw, she watches patiently the full time, then she carefully breaks the shell, and the young chickens come out.

The lambs just dropped are in the field, they totter by the side of their dams, their young limbs can hardly support their weight. If you fall, little lambs, you will not be hurt; there is spread under you a carpet of soft grass; it is spread on purpose to receive you.

The butterflies flutter from bush to bush and open their wings to the warm sun.

The young animals of every kind are sporting about, they feel themselves happy, they are glad to be alive,—they thank Him that has made them alive.

They may thank Him in their hearts, but we can thank Him with our tongues; we are better than they, and can praise Him better.

The birds can warble and the young lambs can bleat, but we can open our lips in His praise, we can speak of all His goodness.

Therefore we will thank Him for ourselves, and we will thank Him for those that cannot speak.

Trees that blossom and little lambs that skip about, if you could, you would say how good He is; but you are silent, we will say it for you.

We will not offer you in sacrifice, but we will offer sacrifice for you; on every hill and in every green field, we will offer the sacrifice of thanksgiving, and the incense of praise.

HYMN III.

Behold the shepherd of the flock, he takes care for his sheep, he leads them among clear brooks, he guides them to fresh pasture: if the young lambs are weary, he carries them in his arms; if they wander, he brings them back.

But who is the shepherd's Shepherd? who takes care for him? who guides him in the path he should go? and, if he wanders, who shall bring him back? God is the shepherd's Shepherd. He is the Shepherd over all; He takes care for all; the whole earth is His fold; we are all His flock; and every herb, and every green field, is the pasture which He has prepared for us.

The mother loves her little child; she brings it up on her knees; she nourishes its body with food; she feeds its mind with knowledge; if it is sick, she nurses it with tender love; she watches over it when asleep; she forgets it not for a moment; she teaches it how to be good; she rejoices daily in its growth.

But who is the Parent of the mother? who nourishes her with good things, and watches over her with tender love, and remembers her every moment? Whose arms are about her to guard her from harm? and if she is sick, who shall heal her?

God is the Parent of the mother; He is the Parent of all, for He created all. All the men and all the women, who are alive in the wide world, are His creation; He loves all, He is good to all.

The king governs his people; he has a golden crown upon his head, and the royal scepter is in his hand; he sits upon a throne, and sends forth his demands; his subjects fear before him: if they

do well, he protects them from danger; and if they do evil, he punishes them.

But who is the Sovereign of the king? who commands him what he must do? whose hand is reached out to protect him from danger? and if he does evil, who shall punish him?

God is the Sovereign of the king; His crown is of rays of light, and His throne is among the stars. He is King of kings, and Lord of lords: if He bids us live, we live; and if He bids us die, we die; His dominion is over all worlds, and the light of His countenance is upon all His works.

God is our Shepherd, therefore we will follow Him; God is our Father, therefore we will love Him; God is our King, therefore we will obey Him.

HYMN IV.

Come, and I will show you what is beautiful. It is a rose in full bloom. See how she sits upon her mossy stem, like the queen of all the flowers! her leaves glow like fire: the air is filled with her sweet odor; she is the delight of every eye.

She is beautiful, but there is a fairer than she. He that made the rose is more beautiful than the rose; He is all lovely; He is the delight of every heart.

I will show you what is strong. The lion is strong; when he raises up himself from his lair, when he shakes his mane, when the voice of his roaring is heard, the cattle of the field fly, and the wild beasts of the desert hide themselves, for he is very terrible.

The lion is strong, but He that made the lion is stronger than he: His anger is terrible: He could make us die in a moment, and no one could save us out of His hand.

I will show you what is glorious. The sun is glorious. When he shines in the clear sky, when he sits on the bright throne in the heavens, and looks abroad over all the earth, he is the most excellent and glorious creature the eye can behold.

The sun is glorious, but He that made the sun is more glorious than he. The eye beholds Him not, for His brightness is more dazzling than we could bear.

He sees in all dark places; by night as well as by day; and the light of His countenance is over all His works.

Who is this great Name, and what is He called, that my lips may praise Him?

This great Name is God. He made all things, but He is himself more excellent than all which He hath made: they are beautiful, but He is beauty; they are strong, but He is strength; they are perfect, but He is perfection.

HYMN V.

The glorious sun is set in the west; the night dews fall; and the air, which was sultry, becomes cool.

The flowers fold up their colored leaves; they fold themselves up, and hang their heads on the slender stalk.

The chickens are gathered under the wing of the hen, and are at rest; the hen herself is at rest also.

The little birds have ceased their warbling, they are asleep on the boughs, each one has his head behind his wing.

There is no murmur of bees around the hive, or among the honeyed woodbines; they have done their work, and lie close in their waxen cells.

The sheep rest upon their soft fleeces, and their loud bleating is no more heard among the hills.

There is no sound of a number of voices, or of children at play, or the trampling of busy feet, and of people hurrying to and fro.

The smith's hammer is not heard upon the anvil; nor the harsh saw of the carpenter.

All men are stretched on their quiet beds; and the child sleeps upon the breast of its mother.

Darkness is spread over the skies, and darkness is upon the ground; every eye is shut and every hand is still.

Who takes care of all people when they are sunk in sleep; when they cannot defend themselves, nor see if danger approaches?

There is an eye that never sleeps; there is an eye that sees in dark night as well as in the bright sunshine.

When there is no light of the sun, nor of the moon; when there is no lamp in the house, nor any little star twinkling through the thick clouds; that eye sees everywhere, in all places, and watches continually over all the families of the earth.

The eye that sleeps not is God's; His hand is always stretched out over us.

He made sleep to refresh us when we are weary: He made night that we might sleep in quiet.

As the mother moves about the house with her finger on her lips, and stills every little noise that her infant be not disturbed,—as she draws the curtains around its bed, and shuts out the light from its tender eyes, so God draws the curtains of darkness around us; so He makes all things to be hushed and still, that His large family may sleep in peace.

Laborers, spent with toil, and young children, and every little humming insect, sleep quietly, for God watches over you.

You may sleep, for He never sleeps; you may close your eyes in safety, for His eye is always open to protect you.

When the darkness is passed away, and the beams of the morning sun strike through your eyelids, begin the day with praising God, who has taken care of you through the night.

Flowers, when you open again, spread your leaves, and smell sweet to His praise.

Birds, when you awake, warble your thanks among the green boughs; sing to Him before you sing to your mates.

Let His praise be in our hearts, when we lie down; let His praise be on our lips, when we awake.

HYMN VI.

Child of reason, from where do you come? What has your eye observed, and where has your foot been wandering?

I have been wandering along the meadows in the thick grass; the cattle were feeding around me or reposing in the cool shade; the corn sprung up in the furrows;

the poppy and the harebell grew among the wheat; the fields were bright with summer, and glowing with beauty.

Did you see nothing more? Did you observe nothing besides? Return again, child of reason, for there are greater things than these.—God's handiwork was among the fields; and did you not perceive Him? His beauty was upon the meadows: His smiles enlivened the sunshine.

I have walked through the thick forest; the wind whispered among the trees; the brook fell from the rocks with a pleasant murmur; the squirrel leapt from bough to bough; and the birds sang to each other among the branches.

Did you hear nothing but the murmur of the brook? no whispers but the whispers of the wind? Return again, child of reason, for there are greater things than these.—God's handiwork was among the trees; His voice sounded in the murmur of the water;

His music warbled in the shade; and did you not attend?

I saw the moon rising behind the trees; it was like a lamp of gold. The stars one after another appeared in the clear firmament.

Presently I saw black clouds arise, and roll towards the south; the lightning streamed in thick flashes over the sky; the thunder growled at a distance; it came nearer, and I felt afraid, for it was loud and terrible.

Did your heart feel no terror, but of the thunderbolt? Was there nothing bright and terrible but the lightning? Return, O child of reason, for there are greater things than these.—God's power was in the storm, and did you not perceive Him?

His terrors were abroad, and did not your heart acknowledge Him?

God is in every place; He speaks in every sound we hear; He is seen in all that our eyes behold; nothing, O child of reason, is without God;—let God therefore be in all thy thoughts.

HYMN VII.

Come, let us go into the thick shade, for it is the noon of day, and the summer sun beats hot upon our heads.

The shade is pleasant and cool; the branches meet above our heads, and shut out the sun as with a green curtain; the grass is soft to our feet, and a clear brook washes the roots of the trees.

The sloping bank is covered with flowers; let us lie down upon it; let us throw our limbs on the fresh grass and sleep; for all things are still, and we are quite alone.

The cattle can lie down to sleep in the cool shade, but we can do what is better; we can raise our voices to heaven; we can praise the great God who made us.

He made the warm sun and the cool shade; the trees that grow upwards, and the brooks that run murmuring along. All the things that we see are His work.

Can we raise our voices up to the high heaven? Can we make Him hear who is above the stars? We need not raise our voices to the stars: for He hears us when we only whisper: when we breathe out words softly with a low voice. He that fills the heavens is here also.

May we that are so young speak to Him that always was? May we, that can hardly speak plain, speak to God?

We that are so young are but lately made alive; therefore we should not forget His forming hand who has made us alive. We that cannot speak plain, should lisp out praises to Him who teaches us how to speak, and has opened our silent lips.

When we could not think of Him, He thought of us; before we could ask Him to bless us, He had already given us many blessings.

He fashions our tender limbs, and causes them to grow; He makes us strong, and tall, and nimble.

Every day we are more active than the former day, therefore every day we ought to praise Him better than the former day.

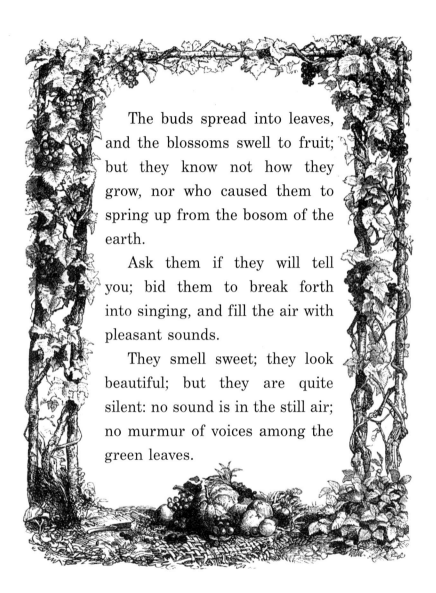

The buds spread into leaves, and the blossoms swell to fruit; but they know not how they grow, nor who caused them to spring up from the bosom of the earth.

Ask them if they will tell you; bid them to break forth into singing, and fill the air with pleasant sounds.

They smell sweet; they look beautiful; but they are quite silent: no sound is in the still air; no murmur of voices among the green leaves.

The plants and the trees are made to give fruit to man; but man is made to praise God who made him.

We love to praise Him, because He loves to bless us; we thank Him for life, because it is a pleasant thing to be alive.

We love God, who has created all beings; we love all beings, because they are the creatures of God.

We cannot be good, as God is good, to all persons everywhere; but we can rejoice that everywhere there is a God to do them good.

We will think of God when we play, and when we work; when we walk out, and when we come in; when we sleep, and when we wake; His praise shall dwell continually upon our lips.

HYMN VIII.

See where stands the cottage of the laborer covered with warm thatch! The mother is spinning at the door; the young children sport before her on the grass; the elder ones learn to labor, and are obedient; the father works to provide them food: either he tills the ground, or he gathers in the corn, or shakes his ripe apples from the tree. His children run to meet him when he comes home, and his wife prepares the wholesome meal.

The father, the mother, and the children make a family; the father is the master thereof. If the family be numerous, and the grounds large, there are servants to help to do the work: all these dwell in one house; they sleep beneath the same roof; they eat the same bread; they kneel down

together and praise God every night and every morning with one voice; they are very closely united, and are dearer to each other than any strangers. If one is sick they mourn together; and if one is happy they rejoice together.

Many houses are built together; many families live near one another; they meet together on the green, and in pleasant walks, and to buy and sell, and in the house of justice: and the sound of the bell calls them to the house of God in company. If one is poor, his neighbor helps him;

if he is sad, he comforts him. This is a village; see where it stands enclosed in a green shade, and the tall spire peeps above the trees.

If there be very many houses, it is a town, it is governed by a magistrate.

Many towns, and a large extent of country, make a kingdom; it is enclosed by mountains; it is divided by rivers; it is washed by seas; the inhabitants thereof are countrymen; they speak the same language; they make war and peace together; a king is the ruler thereof. Many kingdoms and countries full of people, and islands, and large continents, and different climates, make up this whole world—God governs it. The people swarm upon the face of it like ants upon a hillock; some are black with the hot

sun; some cover themselves with furs against the sharp cold; some drink of the fruit of the vine; some the pleasant milk of the coconut, and others quench their thirst with the running stream.

All are God's creation; He knows every one of them, as a shepherd knows his flock; they pray to Him in different languages, but He understands them all; He hears them all; He takes care of all: none are so great that He cannot punish them; none are so poor that He will not protect them.

Poor woman, who sits pining, and weeps over your sick child: though no one sees you, God sees you; though no one pities you, God pities you; raise your voice, forlorn and abandoned one; call upon Him, for assuredly He will hear thee.

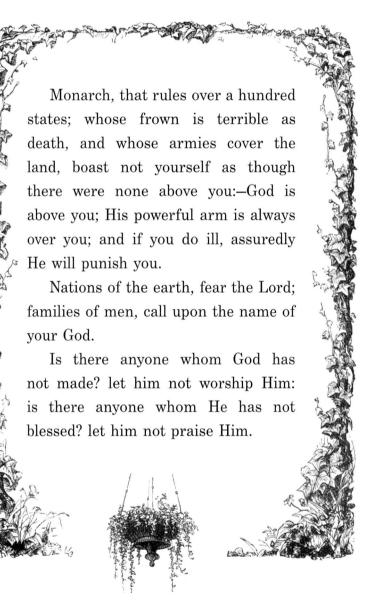

Monarch, that rules over a hundred states; whose frown is terrible as death, and whose armies cover the land, boast not yourself as though there were none above you:—God is above you; His powerful arm is always over you; and if you do ill, assuredly He will punish you.

Nations of the earth, fear the Lord; families of men, call upon the name of your God.

Is there anyone whom God has not made? let him not worship Him: is there anyone whom He has not blessed? let him not praise Him.

HYMN IX.

Come, let us walk abroad; let us talk of the works of God. Take up a handful of sand; number the grains of it; tell them one by one into your lap. Try if you can count the blades of grass in the field, or the leaves on the trees. You cannot count them, they are innumerable; much more the things which God has made.

The fir grows on the high mountain, and the gray willow bends above the stream.

The thistle is armed with
sharp prickles,

the mallow
is soft and
woolly.

The hop lays
hold with her
tendrils, and
clasps the tall
pole; the oak
has firm root
in the ground,
and resists the
winter storm.

The daisy enamels the meadows, and
grows beneath the foot of the passenger.
The tulip asks a rich soil, and the
careful hand of the gardener.

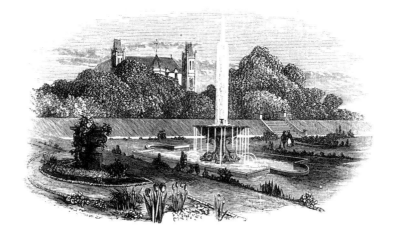

The iris and the reed spring up in the marsh; the rich grass covers the meadows; and the purple heath-flower enlivens the waste ground.

The water-lilies grow beneath the stream; their broad leaves float on the surface of the water; the wallflower takes root in the hard stone, and spreads its fragrance among broken ruins.

Every leaf is of a different form; every plant has a separate inhabitant.

Look at the thorns that are white with blossoms, and the flowers that cover the fields, and the plants that are trodden in the green path. The hand of man has not planted them; the sower has not scattered the seeds from his hand, nor the gardener dug a place for them with his spade.

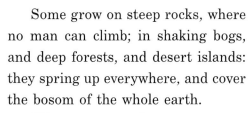

Some grow on steep rocks, where no man can climb; in shaking bogs, and deep forests, and desert islands: they spring up everywhere, and cover the bosom of the whole earth.

Who causes them to grow everywhere, and blows the seeds about in winds, and mixes them with the mold, and waters them with soft rains, and cherishes them with dews? Who fans them with the pure breath of heaven; and gives them colors and smells, and spreads out their thin transparent leaves?

How does the rose draw its crimson from the dark brown earth, or the lily its shining white? How can a small seed contain a plant? How does every plant know its season to put forth? They are marshaled in order: each one knows his place, and stands up in his own rank.

The snow-drop and the primrose make haste to lift their heads above the ground. When the spring comes they say, Here we are. The carnation waits for the full strength of the year; and the hardy laurustinus cheers the winter months.

Every plant produces its like. An ear of corn will not grow from an acorn; nor will a grape-stone produce cherries; but every one springs from its proper seed.

Who preserves them alive through the cold winter, when the snow is on the ground, and the sharp frost bites on the plain? Who sows a small seed, and a little warmth in the bosom of the earth, and causes them to spring up afresh, and sap to rise through the hard fibers?

The trees are withered, naked and bare; they are like dry bones.

Who breathed on them with the breath of spring, and they are covered with verdure, and green leaves sprout from the dead wood?

Lo, these are a part of His works; and a little portion of His wonders. There is little need that I should tell you of God, for everything speaks of Him. Every field is like an open book; every painted flower has a lesson written on its leaves. Every murmuring brook has a tongue; a voice is in every whispering wind.

They all speak of Him who made them; they all tell us, He is very good.

We cannot see God, for He is invisible; but we can see His works. They that know the most will praise God the best; but which of us can number half His works?

HYMN X.

Look at that spreading oak, the pride of the village green: its trunk is massy, its branches are strong. Its roots, like crooked fangs, strike deep into the soil, and support its huge bulk. The birds build among the boughs: the cattle repose beneath its shade: the neighbors form groups beneath the shelter of its green canopy. The old men point it out to their children, but they themselves remember not its growth: generations of men one after another have been born and died, and this son of the forest has remained the same, defying the storms of two hundred winters.

Yet this large tree was once a little acorn; small in size, insignificant in appearance; such as you are now picking up upon the grass beneath it. Such an acorn, whose cup can only contain a drop or two of dew, contained the whole oak. All its massy trunk, all its knotted branches, all its multitude of leaves, were in that acorn; it grew, it spread, it unfolded itself by degrees, it received nourishment from the rain, and the dews, and the well-adapted soil, but it was all there. Rain and dews, and soil, could not raise an oak without the acorn;

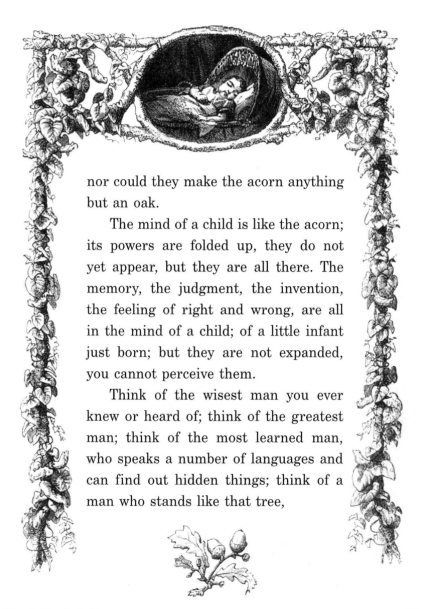

nor could they make the acorn anything
but an oak.

The mind of a child is like the acorn;
its powers are folded up, they do not
yet appear, but they are all there. The
memory, the judgment, the invention,
the feeling of right and wrong, are all
in the mind of a child; of a little infant
just born; but they are not expanded,
you cannot perceive them.

Think of the wisest man you ever
knew or heard of; think of the greatest
man; think of the most learned man,
who speaks a number of languages and
can find out hidden things; think of a
man who stands like that tree,

sheltering and protecting a number of his fellow men, and then say to yourself, the mind of that man was once like mine, his thoughts were childish like my thoughts, nay, he was like the babe just born, which knows nothing, remembers nothing, which cannot distinguish good from evil, nor truth from falsehood.

If you had only seen an acorn, you could never guess at the form and size of an oak; if you had never conversed with a wise man, you could form no idea of him from the mute and helpless infant.

Instruction is the food of the mind; it is like the dew and the rain and the rich soil.

As the soil and the rain and the dew cause the tree to swell and put forth its tender shoots, so do books and study and discourse feed the mind, and make it unfold its hidden powers.

Reverence therefore your own mind; receive the nurture of instruction, that the man within you may grow and flourish. You cannot guess how excellent he may become.

It was long before this oak showed its greatness; year after year passed away, and it had only shot a little way above the ground, a child might have plucked it up with his little hands; it was long before anyone called it a tree; it is long before the child becomes a man.

The acorn might have perished in the ground, the young tree might have been shorn of its graceful boughs, the twig might have bent, and the tree would have been crooked; but if it grew at all, it could have been nothing but an oak, it would not have been grass or flowers, which live their season and then perish from the face of the earth.

The child may be a foolish man, he may be a wicked man, but he must be a man; his nature is not that of any inferior creature, his soul is not akin to the beasts that perish.

O cherish then this precious mind, feed it with truth, nourish it with knowledge; it comes from God, it is made in His image: the oak will last for centuries, but the mind of man is made for immortality.

Respect in the infant the future man.

HYMN XI.

The golden orb of the sun is sunk behind the hills, the colors fade away from the western sky, and the shades of evening fall fast around me.

Deeper and deeper they stretch over the plain; I look at the grass, it is no longer green; the flowers are no more tinted with various hues; the houses, the trees, the cattle, are all lost in the distance. The dark curtain of night is let down over the works of God; they are blotted out from the view as if they were no longer there.

Child of little observation, can you see nothing because you cannot see grass and flowers, trees and cattle? Lift up your eyes from the ground shaded with darkness, to the

heavens that are stretched over your head; see how the stars one by one appear and light up the vast concave. There is the moon bending her bright horns like a silver bow, and shedding her mild light, like liquid silver, over the blue firmament. There is Venus, the evening and morning star; and the

Pleiades, and the Bear that never sets, and the Pole star that guides the mariner over the deep.

Now the mantle of darkness is over the earth; the last little gleam of twilight is faded away; the lights are extinguished in the cottage windows; but the firmament

burns with innumerable fires; every little star twinkles in its place. If you begin to count them they are more than you can number; they are like the sands on the sea shore. The telescope shows you far more, and there are thousands and ten thousands of stars which no telescope has ever reached.

Now Orion heaves his bright shoulder above the horizon, and Sirius, the Dog-star, follows him the brightest of the train.

Look at the Milky Way, it is a field of brightness; its pale light is composed of myriads of burning suns.

All these are God's creation. He gave the sun to shine with a ray of His own glory; He marks the path of the planets, He guides their wanderings through the sky, and traces out their orbit with the finger of His power.

If you were to travel as swift as an arrow from the bow, and to travel on further and further still for millions of years, you would not be out of the creation of God. New suns in the depth of space would still be burning round you, and other planets fulfilling their appointed course.

Lift up your eyes, child of earth, for God has given you a glimpse of heaven. The light of one sun is withdrawn that you may see ten thousand.

Look at the moon when it walks in brightness; gaze at the stars when they are marshaled in the firmament, and adore the Maker of so many worlds.

HYMN XII.

It is now winter, dead winter. Desolation and silence reign in the fields, no singing of birds is heard, no humming of insects. The streams murmur no longer; they are locked up in frost.

The trees lift their naked boughs like withered arms into the bleak sky, the green sap no longer rises in their veins; the flowers and the sweet-smelling shrubs are decayed to their roots.

The sun himself looks cold and cheerless; he gives light only enough to show the universal desolation.

Nature, child of God, mourns for her children. A little while ago and she rejoiced in her offspring: the rose spread its perfume upon the gale; the vine gave its fruit; her children were springing and blooming around her, on every lawn and every green bank.

O Nature, beautiful Nature, beloved child of God, why do you sit mourning and desolate? Has your Father forsaken you? has He left you to perish? Are you no longer the object of His care?

He has not forsaken you, O Nature? you are His beloved child: His own beauty is spread over you, the light of His countenance is shed upon you.

Your children shall live again, they shall spring up and bloom around you; the rose shall again breathe its sweetness on the soft air, and from the bosom of the ground verdure shall spring forth.

For God himself has promised that while the earth remains, seedtime will follow the harvest, and summer will follow the winter.

And you, child of man, look also upon these things and learn.

HYMN XIII.

Child of mortality, from where do you come? why is your countenance sad, and why are your eyes red with weeping?

I have seen the rose in its beauty; it spread its leaves to the morning sun—I returned, it was dying upon its stalk; the grace of the form of it was gone; its loveliness was vanished away; the leaves thereof were scattered on the ground, and no one gathered them again.

A stately tree grew on the plain; its branches were covered with verdure; its boughs spread wide and made a goodly shadow; the trunk was like a strong pillar; the roots were like crooked fangs—I returned, the verdure was nipped by the east wind; the branches were lopped away by the axe; the worm had made its way into the trunk, and the heart thereof was decayed; it moldered away, and fell to the ground.

I have seen insects sporting in the sunshine, and darting along the streams; their wings glittered with gold and purple; their bodies shone like the green emerald: they were more numerous than I could count; their motions were quicker than my eye could glance—I returned, they were brushed into the pool; they were perishing with the evening breeze; the swallow had devoured them; the pike had seized them; there were none found of so great a multitude.

I have seen a man in the pride of his strength; his cheeks glowed with beauty; his limbs were full of activity; he leaped; he walked; he ran; he rejoiced in that he was more excellent than those—I returned, he lay stiff and cold on the bare ground; his feet could no longer move, nor his hands stretch themselves out; his life was departed from him; and therefore do I weep because Death is in the world; the spoiler is among the works of God: all that is made must be destroyed; all that is born must die: let me alone, for I will weep yet longer.

I have seen the flower withering on the stalk, and its bright leaves spread on the ground—I looked again, and it sprang forth afresh; the stem was crowned with new buds, and the sweetness thereof filled the air.

I have seen the sun set in the west, and the shades of night shut in the wide horizon; there was no color, nor shape, nor beauty, nor music; gloom and darkness brooded around—I looked, the sun broke forth again from the east, he gilded the mountain tops; the lark rose to meet him from her low nest, and the shades of darkness fled away.

I have seen the insect, being come to its full size, languish and refuse to eat: it spun itself a tomb, and was shrouded in the silken cone; it lay without feet, or shape, or power to move. I looked again, it had burst its tomb: it was full of life, and sailed on colored wings through the soft air; it rejoiced in its new being.

Thus shall it be with you, O man! and so shall your life be renewed.

Beauty shall spring up out of ashes; and life out of the dust.

A little while you shall lie in the ground, as the seed lies in the bosom of the earth; but you shall be raised again; and if you believe in He who comes, you will never die any more.

Who is He that comes to burst open the prison doors of the tomb, to bid the dead awake and to gather His redeemed from the four winds of heaven?

He descends on a fiery cloud; the sound of a trumpet goes before Him; thousands of angels are on His right hand.

It is Jesus, the Son of God; the Savior of men.

He comes in the glory of His Father; He has received power from on high.

Mourn not, therefore, child of mortality;—for the spoiler, the cruel spoiler, that laid waste the works of God is subdued; Jesus has conquered death: child of immortality! mourn no longer.

HYMN XIV

The rose is sweet, but it is surrounded with thorns; the lily of the valley is fragrant, but it springs up among the brambles. The spring is pleasant, but it is soon past: the summer is bright, but the winter destroys the beauty thereof.

The rainbow is very glorious, but it soon vanishes away: life is good, but it is quickly swallowed up in death.

There is a land, where the roses are without thorns, where the flowers are not mixed with brambles.

In that land there is eternal spring, and light without any cloud.

The tree of life grows in the midst thereof; rivers of pleasures are there, and flowers that never fade.

Myriads of happy spirits are there, and surround the throne of God with a perpetual hymn.

The angels sing praises continually, and the cherubim fly on wings of fire.

This country is Heaven: it is the country of the righteous; and nothing that is wicked must enter there.

The toad must not spit its venom among the turtle doves; nor the poisonous henbane grow among sweet flowers. Neither must anyone that does ill enter into that good land.

This earth is pleasant, for it is God's earth, and it is filled with many delightful things.

But that country is far better; there we shall not grieve any more, nor be sick any more, nor do wrong any more; there the cold of winter shall not wither us, nor the heats of summer scorch us.

In that country there are no wars nor quarrels, but all love one another with dear love.

When our parents and friends die, and are laid in the cold ground, we see them here no more; but there we shall embrace them again, and live with them and be separated no more.

There we shall meet the men of God, whom we read of in the Holy Bible. There we shall see Abraham, the called of God, the father of the faithful; and Moses, after his long wanderings in the desert; and Elijah, the prophet of God; and Daniel, who escaped from the lions' den; and there the son of Jesse, the shepherd king, the sweet singer of Israel. They loved God on earth; they praised Him on earth; but in that country they will praise Him better and love Him more.

There we shall see Jesus, who is gone before us to that happy place; and there we shall behold the glory of the High God. We cannot see Him here, but we will love Him here; we must be now on earth, but we will often think on Heaven.

That happy land is our home; we are to be here but for a little while and there forever, even for ages of eternal years.